THE TENDER BETWEEN

THE TENDER BETWEEN

EVE LUCKRING

ORNITHOPTER PRESS PRINCETON

First Edition
Published by Ornithopter Press
www.ornithopterpress.com

ISBN 978-1-942723-05-9
LCCN 2017917910

Art and design by Mark Harris

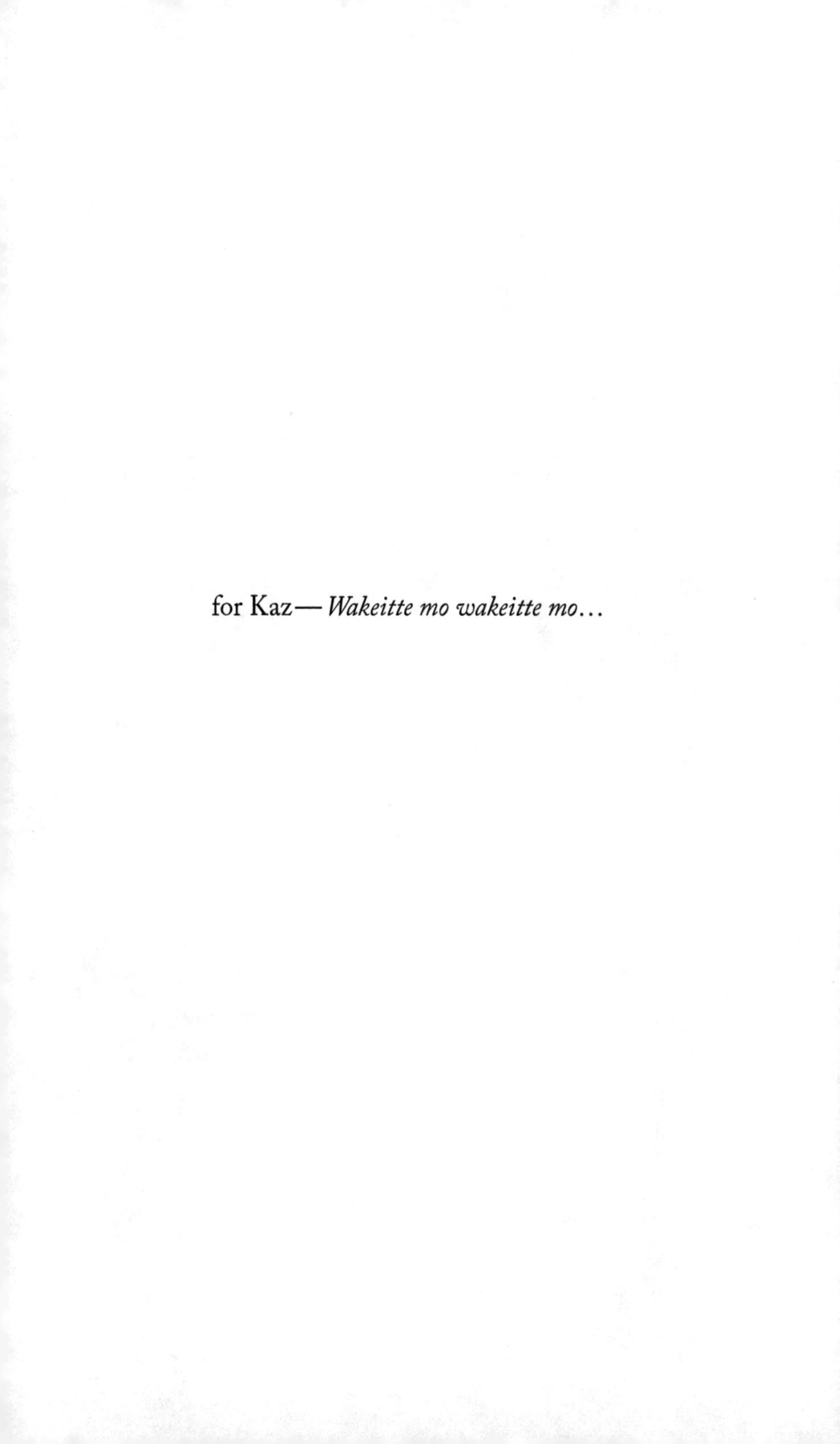

for Kaz—*Wakeitte mo wakeitte mo…*

A person feels so small because he is woven
into nature; he feels so great because he
encompasses all of nature.

—Ogiwara Seisensui

broken bowl
the pieces
still rocking

—Penny Harter

THE TENDER BETWEEN

Becoming,

shelter in a lit match

a moth
a flame
a voice inside my head

matching
this black to that black
crow's caw

creek singing the mind to unthe metallic taste

of what

I can't imagine—

negative tide

in the salt air ~~a memory~~ of speechlessness

half moon
in broad daylight
the placebo effect

I climb a wooden staircase to the top floor of a tall house in a dream.

comin' for
  to carry me…
a circling of moths

Bright under a pitched ceiling, three large windows frame a newborn mountain, jagged from its upheaval out of the sea.

deep in the thrust where another day breaks

I stare a long time at the boulders on the slope. Later, I look up 'mountain' on dreammoods.com. "Many major obstacles and challenges to be overcome. Alternatively, mountains denote a higher realm of consciousness, knowledge, and spiritual truth." Tell me, when speaking of experience, what's the difference?

the mountain submerged
in wind
an old gospel song

a field of grasshoppers camouflaged in delay

hesitating until I'm a hummingbird

to taste
an unnamed nectar
with what tongue

a blank page sheltering the sky

red naked
in a field gone fallow
the finch's song

in tune with

its

ob

st

ac

l

es

rain

present perfect
crow
sheening a pause

Becoming, but for a name—
how can I rebuild what I've never known whole?

"Call me Ishmael," mother reads to me in utero

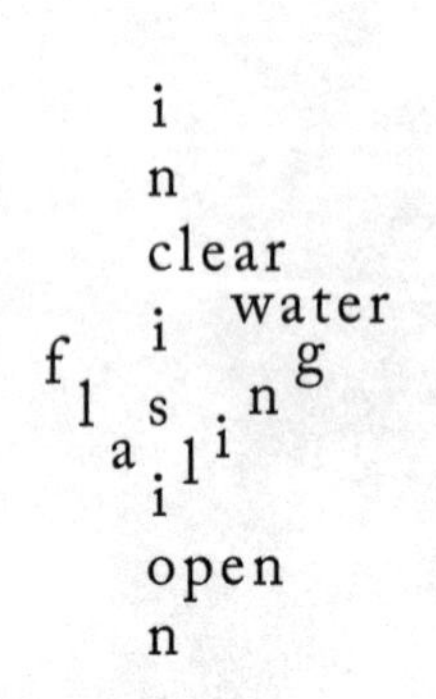

blue moon:
her milk
comes in

swollen
with spring rain
a fairytale in the sandbox

a touch
of breeze, my voice
spills blossoms

wild mustard scent—
a bed
shared with sisters

this side of the equinox this side

salamanders lost to sun on the lips of a dream

a violet picked
not given...
first shrinking

blister moon—
a wish
rubbed raw

I grew up backstage of *Waiting for Godot*, looking for a carrot, like Gogo, dancing for a bone, like Lucky. Stage directions were delivered in curses and prayers, lost boots and black eyes.

The curtain opens to a lone bare-branched tree at nightfall. For me, it always beckons Bashō's famous crow:

枯朶に烏のとまりけり秋の暮
kare eda ni karasu no tomari keri aki no kure

which could be translated as:

on a withered branch
a crow has settled—
autumn evening

A country road. A tree.

for lack of a bit of
crow

sticks and stones... in the beginning was the word

from his rib, she
framed
to shoulder the fall

centuries of whispers, a cathedral beam cracks

cactus bloom:
I decide to forgive
myself

out of the agave
out of the blue
Guadalupe

lily buds—
a Catholic girl
engorged with doubt

or a nun bared to the bone shined night

throbbing stars —
the tilt
of my pelvis

Becoming, but for a name—
how can I rebuild what I've never known whole?

And without a name, what is lost?

open scissors beside a vase of water

F-sharp minor—
a slight swelling
in the wet

dark sea
surging to the brink
of words

near the horizon
a wave forms…
touch me there, again

your kiss deepens midnight's throat of stars

meet me there
behind your eyes
horizonless

a pink
swish
slips
the leaves
a soft moan

the crack in his dream me fluttering

where your eyes attach an old bruise

a long hard lie swells into perjury. spit or swallow?

sore to the touch
his name
in my mouth

words

still pink
close to the bone

Becoming, but for a name—
how can I rebuild what I've never known whole?

And without a name, what is lost?

Is it a story, or a strategy,

As I dress for work, I watch a low cloud gauze the mountain outside my bedroom window.

A crow calls three times from my neighbor's satellite dish. "Here I am—here, here, here."

pine scent in the fear this morning tremors

The sound has the timbre of the earthquake alarm in the building where I teach, but the alarm is higher in pitch, and its incessancy frays the nerves.

What happens when there's no warning of danger; how do we make sense of the surprise attack?

stepping on something tender like territory

Or what if the alarm continually triggers threat, or the memory of it, coursing through the nervous system. An unrelenting state of unease, of waiting for…

maybe in my amygdala maybe a minefield

Qandahar
inside a pomegranate
        ripe cells cleave

photos of Abu Ghraib—
broken blood vessels
in my left brain

fist-first
an oath
of loyalty

hidden for the attack if it is

bleeding under my skin the American Dream

the red legacy of a tool misused

(more than mistaken) “to enhance your safety”

the old names for countries levitating the Pentagon

a generation rips
out the corner
of one eye

so greenly history puts forth thorns

one thousand blades of grass
the taste of a cloudless sky

branches almost bare—
a memory in the colors
of a new bruise

whose blood feeds the marrow
touch
screen

clickbait
the bottom line where your feverdreams tap

always plugged in
always on always
plugged in
ON

sign in!
the back door is open!
free cookies!

licking your lips
swiping, your hands

the accruals of disposable attention spans
in small print side-effects

left ear
right ear
the twisting pitch of an echo chamber

anti-__________

greater-than-or-equal-to your filter bubble

count the sirens' songs, hit delete

and glove what we how

with warmer socks for the morning's disappointments

a complaint
or a prayer

crow,

Becoming, but for a name—
how can I rebuild what I've never known whole?

And without a name, what is lost?

Is it a story, or a strategy,

or something to hold what's missing?

greater-than-or-equal-to a glance back

how it fades in and out of a bus window

diluted before it changes
into a familiar face

less than you know me
less than not enough

less-than-or-equal-to the aisle   your hard stare

the cold times the dark doorway

not an exit (follow the river)

midnight fallen down on her luck

harder than a rock can bump

thinner than whispered   into a cell phone

back
against the wall
cold blade curve of her neck

scoring a behavioral problem in the bathroom

or a black eye passenger-side
for a butter-knife to open the trunk

foiled inside out spit shimmy

an irreducible fraction of a woman dividing by zero

new moon—
a clean place to lay
a discarded name

blackbirds, but they're not

not talking to you, crow

Becoming, but for a name—
how can I rebuild what I've never known whole?

And without a name, what is lost?

Is it a story, or a strategy,

or something to hold what's missing?

These contours, are they me or we,
"the same source but different names"?

sham shiny pennies
us and them

notwithstanding a fourth quarter collateral harvest

stock market crash:
the calculus
of strangers

less-than-or-equal-to less than before

you need a shell company
maybe a conch

or a courtyard hedged in hotel-shaped financial instruments

a zero-sum coyote, probable drought

as long as the table as long as you want

hunger in the spoon

a cornucopia of chlorpyrifos, how to sing it?

bent-back picking a green dream

dusk artificially orange with fragrance

annuals growing blue sky margins from ~~seed~~™

leveraged by a downed beehive swapped at the close

a forest forgotten
a river owed
a smiling cow on the label

until trees can be landlords

(a sycamore leaf falls from the book

here, a crow flies off the page)

An old friend and I sit near a large window in a sun-filled café. I am not aware of the electric lights above each table until they blink off. Simultaneously the music stutters and cuts out.

where a beetle leg twitches golden the quiet

It is barely twenty seconds before the lights come back on and the music returns. No one seems to notice. In the distance a siren sounds. It surges closer and flares red through the room. The overhead lights go off again. This time they do not come back on. Another siren sears by, and another…

in the darkplay
of wingspan
a hollowed vowel

Later that night, my friend emails me a news report: "Nearly 14,000 Mid-Wilshire DWP customers are without power Friday afternoon after a crow flew into electrical equipment, sending the neighborhood into a blackout. When the fire department arrived they found smoke, but no fire."

ashasash

moonrise burying the embers

moths gather
your unfinished business
at my front door

fern tremble   voices small in the distance

soft

in the
col
lapse
of a
star

heels
clicking

Becoming, but for a name—
how can I rebuild what I've never known whole?

And without a name, what is lost?

Is it a story, or a strategy,

or something to hold what's missing?

These contours, are they me or we,
"the same source but different names?"

Beyond reach, a shape shimmers and dissolves...
its reflection rearranges itself

snow through teeth in
the window a glass

the withering wind
porous, our humming

ears ringing—
a hundred black centipedes
and those small bones

of flesh
I have fed
something like a shadow

swallowtail
swallowtail
we all fall down

< a cat
> a carcass
―――――――――
28 flies

part maggot
part bone
part prayer

in the skin of a tiger stalking the tender between

claws re-sheathed the waning moon

taught to hide
in the hollow
of the wind

black on black, I crawl in—

at the edge of the sea entering the barely there

wherein the foghorn a threshold

halflight—
a color between
flesh and bone

inside a bat's ear
a rose
opens to a star

shedding night wingless into the next

as if a lottery ticket and then

NOTES

The Ogiwara Seisensui epigraph was translated by Makoto Ueda.

Penny Harter's poem is from *In The Broken Curve,* Burnt Lake Press, ©1984 Penny Harter, by permission of the author.

The Japanese rendering of Bashō's poem is from Gabi Greve's World Kigo Database. There are multiple versions of this haiku.

"the same source, but different names" is from a translation of Lao-Tzu's *Tao Te Ching* by Stephen Addiss and Stanley Lombardo.

ACKNOWLEDGEMENTS

Many thanks to the editors/jurors of the following publications and contests where most of these poems (often in different versions) first appeared: *A Hundred Gourds, Bones, ant ant ant ant ant, Close to the Wind, Frogpond,* HaikuNow! Contest 2011, *Issa's Untidy Hut,* 16th Annual Kusamakura International Haiku Competition, *Lilliput Review, NOON: journal of the short poem, Mariposa, Modern Haiku, Roadrunner, Scent of Rain,* and *The Heron's Nest.*

Thank you to the handful of readers who offered guidance on early drafts of this venture, and to Susan Silton, for her expertise at the end of the trail. Special thanks to Mady Schutzman whose encouragement and feedback illuminated a path from beginning to end, and helped me recognize several turns along the way. My deepest gratitude to Mark Harris for his sensitivity, astute insights, and commitment to the process. I am indebted to him for the rich dialogue that transformed the raw manuscript into this book.

CPSIA information can be obtained
at www.ICGtesting.com
Printed in the USA
LVHW042344230723
753218LV00004B/548